Forewc

By Daniel Alarik

Your first few months in the military you were drinking from a fire hose of new experiences. You had to relearn how to speak, walk, exercise, shoot weapons and even understand the hierarchical rank structure. But after a few months, things slowly started to normalize and you became comfortable. You could speak the language, workout, and navigate complex new systems so well, you were even helping out the new 'boots'. You went from the foreigner to fluent in 6 months.

Now it's time for you to do it again. But there's one big difference. The guarantee of a paycheck from your days in the military is now gone. The feeling of navigating this unknown of a future career can be daunting.

In some ways you may feel like you are lost in the wilderness. You now lost your map (the comfort of rank and military style career progression), you've lost your compass (your military leadership and mentors), and now you've lost your ruck sack of supplies in case of emergency (everything from the guarantee of a paycheck on the 1st and the 15th to the 3 meals a day).

So now what?

I can tell you from my personal experience of leaving a very disciplined environment of Drill Sergeant duty to becoming a civilian was neither smooth nor comfortable. But I can also tell you that there are tools out there to help you navigate your course.

First and foremost you must absolutely quantify and write down what your goal is in your next chapter in life. This can be as simply stated as:

"On my last day in the military, I will have accepted a job offer in the career of my choosing that can provide for my family in money, healthcare and benefits."

This is a great start but quickly you're going to realize that you might not have the education to get started and much worse, you don't even know how to get your foot into the door for that job.

Seventy percent of jobs are found due to networking or through someone you know. This would most likely leave you at quite the disadvantage as you've been spending the last few years serving our country.

What Matt has been able to do is give you the compass on your journey to your next chapter. LinkedIn is one of the most mis-understood tools by military members for their future careers. It is the ability to quickly and accurately network in a world that you NEED to be in. Matt explains how you can help use this tool to map out your next steps BEFORE you leave and then who you need to reach out to so that you can land a career, not a job.

Your military chapter is about over now, but the book isn't finished. Your next chapter is going to be exciting, and learning the right tools to navigate it will keep you on course not to just provide for yourself and family but to thrive.

 *Daniel Alarik is the founder and chief executive officer of Grunt Style, Alpha Outpost, Grunt Fit, and American Grit. He is the co-founder of Merica Bourbon.*

Contents

Contents

CHAPTER ONE

The Road Ahead

Dear veteran,

Welcome to your new life. It's somewhat difficult and challenging but also filled with tremendous opportunities.

The civilian world, especially for those of you who have spent 20 years or more in the service of your country, is so very different than your time in uniform.

Some of those civilians you'll face have some interesting, but unfounded concepts about your time in uniform. Sadly, there are some who fear you because they believe everyone has some form of PTSD. Others are scared because you have demonstrated leadership, sometimes under fire, and they fear you're going to take their job.

The transition from the military to the civilian world is such that you have to always remember your first day in basic training, a military academy or a ROTC summer camp. If you can remember the humility needed to overcome those first days with a drill sergeant or upper classmen screaming in your ear, you can easily succeed in this transition.

If you remember those early days, you remember how the military formed you into a tribe of brothers and sisters. The military taught you to recognize that working together, you can accomplish anything.

Now, you have to form a new tribe. The skills taught to you in the military will help you in your new life. In the military, you recognized people such as the classic bullshitter and the guy who always looked good in uniform but could never perform basic duties. Your civilian tribe will have people just like them. You have an advantage now in that you can quickly recognize them. During your transition, you can find those comrades or as my Navy pals call them "shipmates," who will help you grow in your new career.

LinkedIn provides a great way to build your new tribe. In this book, we'll help you discover the ways to find the key people who can help with a career transition. Like the groups you built in basic training, they'll help you find hidden job opportunities as well as advise you on the best way to get the formal training needed to move to new opportunities.

So, let's get started, shall we?

CHAPTER TWO

The Journey Ahead

Military professionals typically work very diligently to support their mission. In today's U.S. military, many have spent two to three tours in Afghanistan or Iraq. The return home is filled with the challenge of adjusting to somewhat normal social, family and professional settings.

The day will come when people will separate or retire from the 'other' settings. Having worked with transitioning vets, I have seen many just begin to embrace their path towards a new career at the moment of their retirement ceremony. Unless you have a rich uncle, like Disney's Uncle Scrooge, waiting to hand you a job after your retirement from the military, you will have to find a new job or a new career, likely sooner than you had planned.

I'm hoping that if you are at this part of the book, ideally you still have at least 18 months of military duty before the transition journey begins. Alongside your normal duty requirements, that gives you the time not only to build a proper profile, but also to add a network and truly discover the opportunities and programs available

Consider using the military's transition programs that provide departing forces with professional certifications that certify your hard-earned capabilities. If someone truly wants to stay in aviation repair, for example, the military has educational programs that provide the FAA certifications needed to work in aviation.

An Air Force or Navy crew chief may have launched or repaired many different aircraft. On paper, that looks great. Yet, the FAA certification will be the proof that the crew chief has the desired and required skills that the civilian industry will demand.

As a research tool, LinkedIn can help transitioning vets to determine the job qualifications and certifications needed to jump from a military airfield or flight deck to a commercial setting. Through this social media portal, a crew chief can find other former aircraft mechanics and airfield managers by searching for those terms.

Once they find someone with similar qualifications, it is important to connect with them as soon as possible and tell them the purpose of the contact. For example, consider this as a possible way to share the reason for your request to connect:

> *"Hi Susan. Through LinkedIn, I noted our similar work experience as an avionics repair professional. I am hoping to continue in this line of work when I leave the Air Force, and I hope you'll accept my request so I may learn from you."*

I have found that when someone uses a stated purpose in their connection messaging, people will respond very positively. Military people, once they have left, always support others in sharing information. The same is true for non-military connections. Properly addressed, people will do what they can to help someone get the information needed.

Making a career change

What about that military person who wants to change to another career? Let's start with an Air Force Master Sergeant who spent his years of military service  uploading and supervising **munitions load teams on fighter aircraft.** There isn't much call for that kind of specific skill set, unless somebody wants to train other foreign military forces, and likely live in harsh climates.

In this scenario, let's call this person Mike Jones. Jones has no desire to return to the Middle East after a tour of duty in Kuwait. He wants to explore other options such as information security. At a military job fair, Jones discovers two technical education programs that qualify for VA funding. Both program representatives assure him that the industry is looking for graduates from their programs.

I have seen these program sales professionals at work, and some remind me of the last trip I took to an auto dealership to buy my wife a new Honda. LinkedIn can help Jones past the glossy photos and the quotes of recent graduates from their programs.

If I were in Mike Jones' shoes, I would ask the program marketing representatives for names of recent graduates. If the program indeed has successful graduates, finding one of those graduates will enable Jones to have a better chance at success. A connection with that person on LinkedIn will help Jones, a transitioning military professional like you, find the truth behind the advertised programs.

Continuing this scenario, Jones learns that one school includes a technical writing program as part of their curriculum. However, for someone with Jones' experience, it may not be needed. Through his connection with that graduate, Jones may learn that he can bypass the program and move faster through the curriculum. His new connection tells him how to take the test that will shorten his time in the program.

Unfortunately, Jones also learns that the school doesn't offer the professional certification accreditation as part of the curriculum. The VA does provide the funding for the test, however, and the curriculum provides most of the required education. His new connection tells him where to find the rest of the information that he can study through another online resource.

Still using LinkedIn, Sergeant Jones finds two graduates of the other veteran-based program. He reaches out to them and finds that both successfully completed the program and had a job that paid well for entry-level workers. One of those new connections knows several of Jones' colleagues from the military, and she tells him that her firm is always looking for former military professionals who still have their security clearances.

Removing the smoke and mirrors

What we know is that when properly used as a research tool, LinkedIn can remove the smoke and mirrors that some veterans training programs do not clear away for prospective students. If the vets, who are using their educational transition benefits, research LinkedIn like someone who studies a Consumer Reports article to pick his new truck, they will find an easier transition, especially when they understand and complete the requirements for certifications.

Let's go back to my reasoning for a military professional like Jones to begin his transition efforts 18 months before retirement. If he budgets two hours per week to research career options that interest him, with a year and a half to go he has the time to fully research the best academic or training fit for him. However, imagine if he waited until two months before his retirement. In a rushed mode, he may not have the time to pick the best program for his transition path, or his preferred or most suitable program might not be available.

LinkedIn provides an independent research resource for every transitioning professional, and former and retired military people are particularly connected. Non-military types may not fully understand this, but the "time in uniform" significantly enhances our ability to get the straight scoop. From experience, and from the many I have already helped with their profile, I know that service time will open avenues not as readily available to others. Nonetheless, military professionals must start at the 18-month point to make the connections needed to find transition answers and potential career opportunities.

Somewhere in those last 18 months, military members are required to attend a mandatory transition program where LinkedIn is presented as a marketing tool. Like many government programs, the transition class, or TAP as the students call it, is based on a premise to help people properly and successfully transition to civilian life and careers.

In 1992, I set up one of the military transition pilot programs at Lowry AFB in Colorado. Many of you were born after this event, while others were just joining the military. With the end of Desert Storm One, many military professionals were given new orders - to find a new career – and our mission was to fast track that transition. One guy had orders to a prestigious military officer development course, but his commander had to release him. Another person released was a single mother with 10 years of service. She had no previous plans to opt out, and no sufficient lead time to make beneficial plans.

As the person in charge of community outreach, my job was to help our local community members learn more about these people and the capabilities they have. After creating a job fair, our Lowry transition team initiated a program aimed at helping military professionals with the basics of a resume and proper executive attire. Sitting with Colonel Charlie Cotter one morning on the KOA Mike Rosen radio show, about two weeks before that first job fair, I remember call after call asking how people could take part in this transition program or, in some cases, to offer a job. We had done our job.

Times change. Five years later, it was my turn to go to a transition class. In that short amount of time, every base had implemented a transition program, but my class wasn't the same as before. I had left the initial transition program wondering what the program managers had thought, and what they would change when it came time to expand the effort to other bases. My question was answered as I

listened to two former military briefers read slides provided for them. Neither of the two presenters for our class had any outside experience in finding a job. Both had apparently qualified for the new transition team because they could read the slides to us. If someone asked a relevant question, they did not answer it well at all.

About five years ago, in the evolution of the TAP program, the services added a LinkedIn session. One of my former military LinkedIn students, an Army officer injured in Iraq, shared his impression that the program might well have been labeled: "Death by Transition."

It is not my intent to berate the military TAP program. My goal is to offer some valuable context to what military professionals might have learned in that class.

It's my goal, that by the time you finish the book, and make changes to your profile, you'll know that you have invested your time and effort in a worthwhile endeavor.

Let's get started.

AN 18 MONTH LINKEDIN TRANSITION PLANNING GUIDE

18 months to separation

This is the time to create a LinkedIn profile. When setting it up, make sure to use a non-military email account for notifications. Also, visit your education office to learn about professional certification classes to add to your profile.

17 months to separation

After completing your profile, reach out to other military colleagues from previous duty stations. It's best to send each one a personalized note.

> Robert,
>
> I'm getting close to my retirement or separation date next year. I have just joined LinkedIn to start building my network of advisors and friends. I noticed from your profile that you're now managing a logistics center, and I would love to know more about what you're doing. Perhaps we can set up a time to talk soon.
>
> Regards,
>
> Tom

16 months to separation

Does your military installation belong to a chamber of commerce? If so, ask the chamber how you can volunteer during off-duty time. Organizations like this can provide one with the opportunity to meet new people who can serve as mentors and job influencers. When meeting new people at the chamber, be sure to ask if you can connect with them.

Susan,

It was nice meeting you at the chamber of commerce mixer last night.
I'm hoping that you would allow me to connect with you on LinkedIn.
Perhaps, we could meet for a cup of coffee sometime so that I can learn
more about your company.

Liz

15 months to separation

For those who want to consider completing a college, master's or law degree, now is the time to start to find military professionals who have also graduated from those programs.

14 months to separation | *tip #1*

Want to find out more about a new career after military service? Consider joining a trade organization such as the International Warehouse Logistics Association, the Council of Supply Chain Management, Chartered Institute of Management Accountants, Institute of Management or the Professional Liability Underwriting Society. Through its research capabilities, LinkedIn can provide you with the opportunity to connect with a local chapter's officers or other key members.

14 months to separation | *tip #2*

LinkedIn offers some great professional courses on a variety of topics. Go to www.linkedin.com/learning to find something that interests you.

13 months to separation | *tip #1*

Does grandma want to know what you want for your birthday or Christmas? Ask for a gift certificate to a photo studio. It's time to change from a military profile picture to a more improved non-military photo. Make sure to wear a conservative blue or black jacket with a tie for men and conservative jewelry for women.

13 months to separation | *tip #2*

Going on vacation? Plan some time to meet with people in a specific industry to expand your LinkedIn network.

12 months to separation

Now is the time to capitalize on LinkedIn's offer for all vets to get their one-year, complimentary Premium update. This service allows you to contact others outside of your network.

11 months to separation

Set aside a minute or two every day to look at the people who review your profile. And, if there is a recruiter or other influencer, write them a note. When you click on this box, LinkedIn will tell you who has visited your profile.

10 months to separation

It's time to schedule an appointment with your commander, first sergeant or supervisor to ask that they write a recommendation about your leadership and management expertise. Tell him or her that they can repurpose the language from your last performance report. If needed, you can help them with the format.

9 months to separation

If your network is starting to grow, look for recruiters who specialize in your specific industry. They can advise on possible job opportunities.

8 months to separation

Did you complete that professional certification or accreditation? Make sure to update your LinkedIn profile to show this important milestone.

7 months to separation

Besides checking those people who are visiting your profile, have you taken

advantage of the LinkedIn messaging system to see who has contacted you? Better yet, have you used one or two of those messages to reach other possible job influencers?

6 months to separation

By now, you have a retirement or separation date. For recruiters, this is a critical date to consider you as a possible candidate especially for future availability.

5 months to separation

Remember those military colleagues from other bases or ships? Now is the time to ask for a recommendation from them about the quality of your work as part of their team.

> Hi Bob,
>
> *Thanks for connecting with me last year. I'm looking at jobs within retail management, and I am hoping that you can write a recommendation for my LinkedIn profile. Could you emphasize my team-building skills as part of the U.S.S. Teddy Roosevelt.*

4 months to separation

If you have joined a civilian professional organization, consider taking a bigger role as an officer.

3 months to separation

If this is your retirement month, invite friends or colleagues from the chamber of commerce to both the formal event as well as the after party. Don't forget to let those new LinkedIn contacts outside of your base know about this with a picture of your retirement event.

2 months to separation

For all of your friends who attended that retirement ceremony and party, follow up with a thank you note and ask to get a time for a cup of coffee.

1 month to separation

Hopefully the next job offer is here or you're awaiting the start of the next semester of college.

A military member's transition may begin with two questions:

1. *Do I really like what I am doing? Can I transfer my skills to something in a non-military setting? What kind of accreditation programs are there to certify my professional experience?*

2. *What if I want to change my career? What type of VA approved training options are available to make that change? And more importantly, what's will the job market be like for me when I complete the training?*

To me, those questions begin the process for starting a **LinkedIn summary statement.** When you have answers to those questions, you can complete the summary. By the way, some elements of the summary will change as you begin to move through the transition.

For those who want to stay in the same career, a LinkedIn summary will help clarify the need for advice and help on the professional accreditation requirements.

Let's go back to the avionics professional. She wants to remain in the industry. She's starting to take the FAA certification programs needed to work on commercial aircraft. She might be best served by a summary like:

"I've been fixing and supervising various aircraft avionics and main-tenance teams throughout my career. I want to remain and grow with the technology in the industry, and to work with other professionals who appreciate the importance of aircraft avionics and maintenance. I am now completing various FAA certification requirements. I am asking that if you already work in this key industry, or know someone who does, that you'll help guide me to determine the right technical education requirements to achieve my goal."

Our hypothetical Sergeant Mike Jones thinks he wants to retrain as an information security professional. His profile might read like this:

"I have been loading and leading munitions load teams on various fighter planes during most of my military career. However, when I retire in 18 months, I will seek a new career. I have an interest in computer programming, and I'm considering information security as an option."

If you work in information security, I ask that you recommend the best information security training options, and the projected certifications that may be available to me after my retirement."

CHAPTER THREE

How your photo makes a first impression

One of the most important things for your LinkedIn profile is your photo. With LinkedIn placing a bigger focus on the mobile features of its platform, there are some key changes that you need to consider.

Before we get to the mobile aspect, let's talk about the need to find a professional photographer. Mark Zamzow, a retired flag officer [3]and one of my clients, went to J.C. Penney's and purchased a professional photo for his profile. The cost was about $75.

Coast Guard Master Chief Judd Reno is using his official photo in his profile. It does show his military professionalism, but here's something to ponder. While the U.S. and Coast Guard flag represent his service, the cynic in me also would have me believe that an human resource professional would offer him a lower-paying job than someone with his leadership talents. Sadly, a lot of non-vets believe that military professionals like Chief Reno have a good income from their pension. That's why, it's important to use a non-military photo for a LinkedIn profile.

Jimmy Bono, another retired Army professional, went to a Centurion Military Alliance non-profit career transition seminar where a photographer was shooting professional photos for each attendee. That was about three months ago, and the promised, complimentary photo for his LinkedIn profile was never sent to him.

If you are transitioning within the next year to 18 months, one of the best gifts that someone could give you for your birthday is a photo shoot with a professional photographer. Portrait studios abound in any community, so the local Wal-Mart and other retailers are a good starting point.

Before going to that studio session, invest in a haircut or visit a local beauty salon. Men who have a five o'clock shadow (like me) need to shave an hour or so before the session. I recommend a black or blue dark suit with a white shirt or blouse.

Army First Sergeant Claudia E. Barros has her profile shot posted in what I would term the "chain of command" wall. Sergeant Barros said her commander terms her photo as "the hammer and soul eater."

If you visited her profile, you would see a different side of her. It shows the non-military side of her capabilities.

After you get a photo, it's time to scan it into a jpeg format. This isn't difficult, but I want to advise you on cropping it for the mobile platform. The photos taken by most studio photographers include the shoulders and a portion of the upper torso. When you're sitting for a portrait, ask the photographer to tighten his lens to capture your head and the neck only. When you upload this into your profile, the photo, with these focused features, will "pop" on a mobile device. This is the most effective because, as the HR staff screens your completed profile, most of them will use a desktop computer to review your information.

However, more and more of us are using an Iphone or Android phone to look at a profile. If you are meeting a mentor or another 'center of influence' for the first time at their office, or for coffee or breakfast, they'll probably look at your profile on a mobile device. Having that highly cropped photo will help them easily find you for that critical first-time meeting.

As a stopgap process, if you cannot get to a professional photographer, I would suggest asking someone with a single lens reflex camera to shoot your photo against a neutral background. A gray or white wall will work. The output should be at least 300 DPI (digital pixels per inch). Then, when grandma, or someone else who loves you, gives you that birthday gift of a photo session, you can update your profile picture with a professional portrait.

Many active duty professionals consider their military photo as an option for LinkedIn. If you have that photo, and you're a commander, first sergeant or supervisor, I would bet you have that classic gritted teeth look of the late John Wayne. That's the photo that conveys to others under your command that you're a serious military leader.

Mark, a former base commander at an Oklahoma installation, showed me his friendly approachable photo, and then another one that reminded me of the many commanders I knew during my 20-year tenure at Air Force bases. The second photo reminded me of one my favorite wing commanders, Lt. Gen. Claudius "Buzz" Watts. General Watts served as the 63rd Military Airlift Wing Commander. His junior enlisted staff saw that official photo and understood that

As my wing commander, General Claudius (Bud) E. Watts mastered the art of walking around. He was a warm, but no-nonsense type who had a commander photo that conveyed to everyone that one could find him showing up at anytime in your off-duty and duty day. And, if you weren't up to his high standards, he would let you quietly know about it.

if they got into trouble, he was going to bust them. However, as Colonel Watts' base newspaper editor, I had talked to him often enough to know he could convey a warmer side. Yet, when it came to safety, and driving under the influence, my former wing commander had a very strict demeanor, and his official photo reflected just that. Choose your photo wisely.

Before uploading your choice of photos, I would ask your spouse, trusted friend or colleagues which photo is the better one to convey your professionalism. As someone who advises business leaders and those in my extended military family, the photo acts as a starting point in making a positive impression of your capabilities.

CHAPTER FOUR

The Hidden Headline

Auto executive Lee Iacocca noted that the most powerful person at his college newspaper was the headline writer.

As any journalist knows, a great headline helps readers understand the purpose of any article. However, in a world where people are bombarded with never ending "headers" on their phone, computer, or tablets, it's important to recognize that this key aspect of any article is often poorly done.

When setting up your LinkedIn profile, everyone gets a chance to write their own headline as the initial part of their LinkedIn profile. Too often, transitioning military professionals overlook the marketing aspects of this LinkedIn element. Like the many forms they had to complete, military professionals put whatever comes to mind with the term "transitioning" as part of the headline. Most military professionals do not grasp that the header can help educate a possible employer or a center of influence on their aspirations.

Willie Ford, an IT professional who spent seven years in the Air Force, represented the type of headlines most transitioning military professionals use. He used something probably taken from the Department of Labor transition guide where some government bureaucrat thought the transitioning term was needed in the header.

As his LinkedIn coach, I knew Willie was given a lot of responsibility when he first reported for duty as an airman at Maxwell AFB, Alabama. Working in a computer support section, his boss, a retired Air Force lieutenant colonel, gave him the duties of a technical sergeant. In his first assignment, Willie actually served as a project manager, directing others more senior in rank, to complete IT projects. Now, Willie's LinkedIn headline reads "Willie S. Ford, IT Program Manager. Finding solutions for complex tech issues."

Rod Greensage, a social media marketing colleague, showed me what some would term an "Easter Egg" for the headline section when he and I presented a LinkedIn class several months ago. You can double the headline space given by putting both your first and last name in the "first name" box of the profile. In the last name box, you can then put a smaller headline. Rod's first header placed "Social Media Marketing" in his last name.

He then placed "Lead Generation Expert Providing Clients Targeted Leads via Facebook Marketing & Other Popular Social Media Platforms" as his second headline. To me, this LinkedIn headline represents the gold standard of how to write a headline for this platform. Another important element when using this Easter Egg is to use a comma after your full name in the first name of the header. This gives a reader a short break.

Another key aspect to updating one's LinkedIn header is the use of a middle initial or a nickname. Many of us believe we're the only one with our name with a profile on LinkedIn. If you don't believe me, trying search for "Matt Scherer" on LinkedIn. I did, and I found about six or seven of them from various parts of the world.

My given name is David Matthew Scherer. The only people who used that name was my late mother, my spouse when she's angry, and of course every Catholic nun I had in grammar school. During those eight years, they either used the "David Matthew" or the "Matthew" when I wasn't paying attention or causing mischief.

Once I understood that there were others with my name, I changed my profile to D. Matt Scherer. If I meet someone I want to connect with, I tell them to look for that moniker. So, don't forget the middle (or first!) initial when updating your LinkedIn profile.

Once you have those two headlines, check how your profile appears in a mobile platform like your phone or tablet. Research is showing that over 60-percent of us access LinkedIn in this format. The well written, two elements headline is such that it conveys your talents; having two of them makes your profile really "pop" on the phone.

LinkedIn headlines capabilities are such that they give each profile user a chance to highlight your talents and skills. Those transitioning military professionals who take the time to consider these elements, and to convey them in their profile, will make a better impression than those who still keep the dreary "transitioning military professional" as part of their headline. Changing your headline is both simple and highly effective.

A good LinkedIn headline can be broken down into three parts: name, job title, and a brief summary that catches the eye.

1. Name: In the First Name box [1] you will want to put your first name. You should include your middle initial as a way of distinguishing yourself from others who share your name.

2. Job Title: In the Last Name box [2] you will want to put your current job title. This nifty trick will increase your chances of getting noticed by prospective employers.

3. Summary: In the Headline Box [3], write a five to seven-word phrase that sums up your goals and ambitions.

CHAPTER FIVE

That LinkedIn summary

When working with military veterans on setting up their LinkedIn profile, I find many don't understand how to express the two to three things that define their unique value proposition. I created a page in a LinkedIn instructional work book where I have left an almost blank page listing the numbers, one, two and three. My goal through that page is to have vets formulate the three things that make them unique and enables them to frame their goals for their LinkedIn summary.

Many express themselves with those hackneyed and over-used terms - "dynamic" as their first choice, and "self-driven" as their second choice. Everybody else is the same.

I understand that many vets have never had to really think through or express their uniqueness. For the most part, the status in their career doesn't matter. I've worked with college students as well as business professionals and many of

them also use those LinkedIn summary buzzwords. It takes some time to develop the ideas of what their mission status is, and what their willingness to work is. So, just how can you overcome that willingness to mimic others and use those trite adjectives to describe your talent and value?

Working with military professionals, I see most in three categories when they leave the military. For some, a military transition involves further education and training. For others, they loved what they did in the military so much that they want to continue it after completing their duty obligations. Still others want to explore other career options.

If someone wants to change careers after leaving the military, these three internal questions should make up part of the decision process for the **three points needed in one's summary.**

1. *What career change interests you?*

2. *What are the courses and certifications needed to get a job in that industry?*

3. *Who is a fellow vet who has done that, or has a relative or trusted friend who can help find the best academic course towards success?*

Let's take Bill who is interested in a career in plumbing. **On his goal sheet, he could put down these three points:**

1. *I am interested in plumbing, but I'm not sure if I want to work as an "on call" plumber or a commercial one who installs sewer and water pipes for homes or other construction.*

2. *What are the best ways to find courses that will use my VA benefits to help me complete entry-level training?*

3. *Is there someone I can talk to about these courses?*

If Bill had asked me to help him with his summary, I would suggest something like this:

> *"I'm leaving the Navy after five years of service. My background was in communications, but I'm interested in becoming a plumber. I'm looking for help in finding the right certification programs and someone to talk to who may have taken similar programs. If you can help me get answers to those questions, please contact me."*

Bill has an aunt who works as an operations manager for a mid-sized air conditioning repair firm. After reading his updated summary, she sends his profile to a colleague who specializes in building new homes. Recognizing Bill's need to get some helpful advice, the new homebuilder reaches out to him to set up a phone meeting.

That's the power of that type of LinkedIn summaries. For the Bills and the others in his military family, the summary shares their vision statement.

Many younger military professionals understand that completing their military service enables them to go back to college to pursue a career. LinkedIn allows these military professionals the opportunity to share their academic vision.

For those who want to express this on their LinkedIn summary, consider Joan, an Army vet who spent her four years of service as a tank mechanic. Jill writes down these **goals as part of her LinkedIn summary:**

Goal #1: *I want to go to law school. I have 75 hours of credit earned before I entered the military along with the after hours classes I took during my military service.*

Goal #2: *My spouse wants to stay in the Dallas-Fort Worth area. So, I want to find the right undergraduate and postgraduate courses of study.*

Goal #3: *As a minority, I might qualify for some academic grants, especially with a 3.9 GPA for the 12 classes I completed during my military service.*

Here's what she might write as **her LinkedIn summary:**

"I am set to leave the military in nine months, and I know I want to go to law school with my VA educational benefits. I'm very interested in criminal defense after I complete my law degree. My educational counselors tell me that with a 3.9 GPA, and with my minority heritage, I might find academic scholarships to support my studies. If you, or someone you know, can help me find the best schools in the Dallas-Fort Worth area, please call me."

Once that's completed, Joan can find other military professionals who have attended pre-law and law school in North Texas. Having this summary in place can help her connect with those who served in the military and also capitalized on their educational benefits. (Note:we'll cover the research and development opportunities of LinkedIn in a future chapter.)

CHAPTER SIX
Beware the use of ResumeSpeak

Through almost a decade on LinkedIn, and interacting with others through this social media portal, I sense that most career transition novices believe that once they add a profile, it's time to post their resume.

For military veterans, the use of what I term "resumespeak" is the method used to fill out a job application, or one of those forms for the Joint Hometown News Service program. By using a resume, perhaps started as part of the transition program, or one developed through other military channels, a veteran is led to believe that his or her profile will attract the attention of people who are looking to hire them.

The LinkedIn profile acts as a beacon in a world where staffing and human resource professionals are looking for qualified professionals. Transition workshops often encourage and express that thought process.

That kind of thinking is typical, but, in my decade of opinion and success, what the folks from the Department of Labor present, as well as their contract teams, is not correct. I want to give you a perspective about these instructors.

Several years ago, I was helping a transitioning vet who was leaving the military after injuries. He was in the midst of getting his profile updated when he went to the mandatory TAP session. After hearing his instructor give the LinkedIn presentation, he asked her about her profile and background. That's when he learned she was a former substitute English teacher in El Paso. The TAP instructors will have you believe that using the resume style is the only method by which a recruiter will find you and want to call you for an interview. This singular reumespeak myth also applies to non-profit organizations that help vets with their transition efforts.

When my daughter graduated from her Arkansas college several years ago, I stopped in Dallas to attend a workshop on resumes and LinkedIn. Again, the instructor, a thirty-something English major, was telling a captive audience, twenty or so students, that using "resumespeak" was the only way for every veteran to complete his profile.

Last year, I helped veterans at a monthly USO luncheon with their profiles. One Air Force lieutenant colonel was convinced that his profile style needed to use resumespeak because, as he was advised, the staffing professionals could upload it into their search algorithms. In the course of helping vets update their profile, I have found that is not true.

Most staffing professionals are looking for a compelling story as they look for candidates. Using resumespeak does not meet that requirement. When a staffing professional is serious enough to propose someone as a candidate, it is then that they will ask for the resume.

In the next couple of chapters, I am going to share how to change your resume into the preferred first person, the "I before she" communication style for expressing talents and dreams. As you work through the exercises you receive, please remember that this first person style will work much better in your effort not only to find jobs but, equally, to find important mentors.

Despite a greater success with both "I before she" and resumespeak, some people still write their profiles in the third person. That is always wrong. If anyone believes that style of expression is better, let me suggest this: If you are using some form of Microsoft Word, try the corporate format and have the voice read that back to you with your eyes closed. Now, try the same process in the "I before she" approach. I contend that after that brief exercise, the difference will be apparent, and it will convince you that a first person, story-telling format is better. Recruiters do not want to know about your friend, they want to hear about you.

For many of us who wore the uniform, the transition to the first person style is difficult. It's just not a natural style for most of us. However, think of the language style as a commander giving orders, or better yet, his subordinate clarifying them.

Telling your story will take some time. You will need to enlist the help of others to listen to it. Then you can refine it. In my view, LinkedIn is an evolutionary process where you first adjust to it, then address the changes that will need to make.

Think of your LinkedIn profile as not only a beacon, but once read, an artistic masterpiece that reflects your individual style. After all, you should understand that many others are going to use some of those same, fantastic adjectives in the context of creating their own profiles. The military TAP program personnel and other non-profit organizations, may, perhaps unwittingly, have every vet use the same terms - dynamic, self-driven and other similar great words - to convey your leadership potential. You need to be different.

In the next chapter, I am going to ask you to take some time to think about three things that make you different from others. LinkedIn will provide you the opportunity to tell your story, the one that will truly help you with your career transition.

CHAPTER SEVEN

The LinkedIn Experience

Sometimes, while helping veterans update their LinkedIn profile, I feel like Forrest Gump and his box of chocolates. I don't know what I am going to get in terms of experiences or skills.

When I read most job experience documents for transitioning military professionals, they bring back memories of a wintery Sunday afternoon in Illinois, putting together a 1000-piece jigsaw puzzle with my mother and father. It's both time consuming and rewarding. Sorting through the shapes and colors of the puzzles of reposted resumes for military veterans, I discover hidden, amazing stories.

Such was the case with George. Before his August 2017 retirement, he was the vice commander of an organization with 58 units located worldwide. The experience section of his resume dutifully contained all the usual buzz words. Yet, it wasn't really telling his story.

When I work with military professionals like George, I remind them that the content should convey a saga of their time at any post. With him, I told him about my great aunt, Mildred. Aunty Mill, as my family called her, gave the impression that she was a sweet little old lady who ran the administrative side of my late uncle's business. While she was deceptively sweet, she also had tremendous business acumen. I'm convinced that every transitioning vet may have an elderly relative like mine.

In this chapter, I want everyone to envision such a person, take those resume points, and craft them into the you that they could understand. That's exactly how George repurposed the experience section for his revised LinkedIn profile.

I'm sure if Aunty Mill were alive today, she would understand what George did in his last duties with the Air Force when he posted this:

> *"From division chief of operations support and training, I was promoted to the #2 executive of an organization responsible for command and control of 58 satellite units located around the globe. In this role, I made sure my team of over 450 military and civilians had the right training, best facilities and equipment as well as the direction to do their job. With more than 40% staffing reductions, my team and I met our military mission. We also reorganized the group into one that was more efficient[4]. "*

Having made the updates to his profile, along with his resume, George received another promotion, this time through a smart transition, and he is now working as a senior project manager for a major insurance company.

Corey, an Army noncommissioned officer, had a LinkedIn profile based on ideas from a transition professional who had suggested the kinds of writing that, had Aunty Mill seen it, would have caused her much confusion.

In ten minutes, we reshaped the confusing language and told his story. In Iraq, Corey conducted training for an international team of EOD specialists. His students came from the U.S., Iraq, Great Britain and other NATO nations. The new language in his new profile told that story, and shortly after his LinkedIn update, he was hired for a job that capitalized on his experiences.

When I work with transitioning military professionals, I remind them that the "experience" section should act as the second act for one's background. A summary, the brief information located near one's photo and header, acts like a fishing pal who encourages the reader to go beyond the first hundred or so words - to get the rest of the story.

When military professionals grasp this concept, they then have a networking tool that conveys their capabilities. While working on that section, go visit your elderly aunt, or any relative, and read them your resume. Then change it to one that they can understand.

Remember, one's military career has a story or two that should be shared with potential employers, not to mention the mentors and other influencers who will help with your career transition.

However, having a better profile is just the starting point towards making a LinkedIn profile into something that will effectively help in the ongoing job and career transition networking needed to find your next career.

CHAPTER EIGHT

Getting Recommendations

If I had $5 for every time I saw the words "self-driven" and "dynamic" in transitioning LinkedIn military profiles, I would have enough money to buy some front row seats to see the St. Louis Cardinals play the Chicago Cubs for a three game series. That fund could also pay for first class airfare to any city in the world, and accommodations in one of their best hotels.

As a rule, I'm not against these adjectives. However, there's a better place for them, and certainly within a military professional's LinkedIn profile. That better place is in the recommendations every transitioning vet should get from their supervisors and colleagues. That's where those adjectives should reside.

Let's take the hypothetical case of Julie, a military human resources professional. She supervises three others in managing her squadron's personnel records and training needs. She knows that she likes this kind of work, and, wanting to continue in human resources when she retires, she is working towards her Professional in Human Resources (PHR) certification. Her retirement is six months away. As she completes her profile, it's time for her to ask her commander and first sergeant to give her recommendations about her work.

I have engaged in many polite arguments with others on the protocol of asking a military boss for such recommendations. One colleague said that military professionals should never ever ask for them. To that response, I had a short, less polite, one-word answer that began with the letter "B" and ended with a "t."

Here's one suggested way to get a recommendation from a current commander or supervisor before your retirement or separation from military service. Speak to each of them for five minutes in private. Share a printed copy of your LinkedIn profile, and ask them to write a recommendation about the work you have done. Luddites like my colleague may not understand this approach, but in the current environment, commanders and supervisors will be happy to assist.

Their recommendations act directly as the most relevant embellishments on your story in the LinkedIn experience. All that's needed from a commander or supervisor is to have a LinkedIn profile to which you connect. Then you, the soon departing military professional, can go to the "more" section of their profile to request a recommendation. Alternatively, you can go to your own recommendations section, hit the edit icon, and request the recommendation from them[5].

LinkedIn will forward that request to the commander, asking for a recommendation on your body of work. A smart commander can probably take some aspects of your performance report and repurpose it. Depending on your relationship, a commander might even ask you to draft it. When the recommendation is completed, LinkedIn sends it to you for your permission to use it.

Commanders and other supervisors know that their mission success depended on their team to accomplish it. When the time is right, it's time for them to acknowledge that contribution from those team members by writing a simple recommendation that will help them move to the next phase of their career.

Jody Weiss, an executive staffing consultant, said he looks for these recommendations when he looks at any candidate. Having these pertinent superlatives residing next to an on-line candidate's experience helps professionals like him sell the person to be a C-Suite (chief executive level) officer.

CHAPTER NINE

The art of the purposeful LinkedIn connection

One of the best ways for transitioning veterans to find mentors and job opportunities is by taking an active role in industry organizations. Here in San Antonio, the Alamo chapter of the Professional Management Institute (PMI) represents one of the many types of organizations that can help someone find a path towards a career after military service.

I'm using that organization to make a point about how any active duty military member can reach out, purposefully, to get a quality connection from meeting someone at one of PMI's many events.

In a hypothetical case, Tom, an Army officer with 18 years of military logistics experience, meets Kevin D. Martin, one of the organization's active members, at a local PMI event. He and Kevin have a productive five-minute conversation and exchange business cards. At the end of the conversation, Tom politely asks if Kevin is on LinkedIn, and if he would connect with him on-line. Tom agrees.

The next morning, Tom finds Kevin's profile (it was easy to find with the "D" middle initial). As Tom has a contact or two already connected with Kevin, it's easy to write that connection request.

I tell transitioning military people to remember that not everyone, like my colleague Kevin, may remember much about that first connection at the event. Therefore, it's important to use the 300 characters allowed in a connection request to remind your new connection of the place you met and a little about the conversation. Tom might write:

> *"Kevin. It was great to meet you at the Alamo PMI chapter meeting. We talked about the military based transition programs in PMI, and I appreciated your input. Please accept my request to be a connection."*

As an active LinkedIn participant, I get quite a few requests from people. Not many take the time to write a note or a reason for their connection request. They assume that since we have mutual contacts, that the connection will be automatic. That is not necessarily true, and I do not always accept blind requests. But, the ones that take the two to three minutes to write a note with their request always make a positive impression.

Because he's interested in getting a law degree after his retirement, Tom wants to find attorneys who have gone to law school near his hometown of Buffalo, NY. He locates two or three through a LinkedIn search. With each potential connection, he then writes a note like this:

> *"Hi Clint. I'm retiring from the Army in 18 months, and I am considering law school to start a new career. I noticed in your profile that you graduated from the law school at St. Bonaventure. I'm hoping that we can connect so that I can get your thoughts on their school."*

At this point, Clint doesn't know Tom. Yet, the note that Tom attached to his connection request is such that Clint will more likely be inclined to accept his request. Again, it's my experience that most people will accept a request that contains a stated purpose.

Once people like Clint and Kevin accept a connection, the next step is to use the LinkedIn messaging feature to send a follow on message. I'd recommend something like this:

> *"Kevin, thanks for connecting with me. I hope that we could find some time in the next couple of weeks to have a phone call or meet for coffee. Please let me know what works best for you."*

For those contacts who reside outside of the local community of either connection, I suggest that you set up a "virtual" cup of coffee, a phone call or FaceTime. That tells people that you respect their time and are only asking for 10 to 20 minutes to get some insight and advice regarding careers or post-military education.

Military members should remember that connection requests can take time, especially with busy people. Most do respond within a day, but I have seen some requests take as long as a week. I once had someone accept a connection request after nine months. Nonetheless, one day typifies how long most requests will take, especially the requests that have a stated purpose.

Kevin Shaughnessy, one of my consulting partners, would tell you that purposeful networking will help anyone uncover opportunities. As with Kevin, I strongly believe that if a military professional specifies the reason for connecting, most people will accept the request.

It's always up to you to take that next step by asking to speak with someone on the phone or meet for a cup of coffee. The proof of this proper effort comes when you build a quality network. Not only does a quality network help people in a job search mode, but it also helps to find input on any related challenges they may face in their career transition.

Organizations like PMI, Human Resources Management Association, The International Society of Logistics, and others like them, welcome military members throughout the U.S. and the world. It's up to the transitioning military professional to develop connections with those organizations and the like-minded people who are members of them. A simple online search can create those important and necessary additions to your transition process.

CHAPTER TEN

How to reach other purposeful connections

John Hancock, a buddy of mine, gets a lot of requests from veterans who discover that he works for USAA. Many directly contact John with a LinkedIn request in the hopes that he can put a good word in with the folks who hire for the San Antonio military based insurance company.

Military members are not the only folks who don't understand how "purposeful networking" can help them truly connect with others. There are some alleged LinkedIn sales gurus who work with some financial services companies who teach their new recruits to try to connect with as many people as possible[6]. Somewhere, they teach that there's a magical formula for the number of contacts by reaching out to would-be connections on LinkedIn. If the sales professional obtains this special quota of LinkedIn connections, he or she will get a sale.

Back to my friend, John. He's the kind of guy who will try to help others if he can. Yet, he has nothing to do with hiring   policies at USAA. He has one of the best jobs in that company as he represents them at the Army-Navy game and other sporting events across the country. Some basic research by those transitioning military members would have helped them understand how John can at best point them to the right place to post a resume for jobs at his company.

To me, LinkedIn research starts with the activation of your Premium account. With a basic account, veterans have a limited number of contacts especially for those who are not connected with someone in their list of contacts.

In basic level LinkedIn, a veteran might search for USAA and see only John and the initial of his last name. Without the Premium feature, which costs about $60 a month, LinkedIn prevents you from getting a lot of information.

Here's a good time to explain the first degree, the second degree and the third degree of connection. My friend, John and I are connected as first degree. If you want to connect with all his direct contacts, LinkedIn allows those with a basic service to reach out to them. For example, if you wanted to connect with the hundreds of connections in John's circle, you can do that. However, if there's someone outside of John's 2500 or more connections[7], you must have a second-degree connector between him and that person.

That's why the LinkedIn premium service, available for a year at no charge for military professionals, provides a research tool to expand one's network outside of even the well-connected types like John. For those veterans who are within a year of a transition point – retirement, medical discharge or separation, that's the time to capitalize on the premium service offered to military professionals.

With this service, a transitioning military professional gets 10 inmails [8]that connect with those outside one connection's second degree.

However, military professionals must use these free emails sparingly and with purpose.

Here's where every transitioning vet must define the purpose behind a connection. For example, a young veteran who's working as a Navy mass communications specialist is looking at attending a school that will give him a degree in marketing. He notes from John's profile that he attended the University of Maryland. Seeing this piece of information gives him a purpose for a connection with John.

One way to minimize the LinkedIn premium mail is to connect with a person too. Our transitioning sailor can also ask him to connect as contacts. Let me suggest here that while this a way to conserve those valuable inmails, each must have a purpose to it.

If I was the mass communications specialist in my hypothetical example, I might write this in the 300 characters given me in my connection request.

> *"Hi John, I'm leaving the Navy in 8 months. I saw that you attended Maryland, and I am interested in their degree program. That's why I am asking to connect with you."*

When someone like John agrees to connect, then it's time for a follow-on question about Maryland.

Our Navy mass communications specialist could then follow up with a "Thanks for connecting with me. I do have a question about Maryland and their programs......"

One would hope that a request to connect would happen quickly. Yet, every busy person has a limited amount of time to respond to them. However, having a fully vested profile when connecting or sending an inmail will help expand one's contacts.

Having a purpose to any LinkedIn request begins the slow process towards building contacts that can aid in the job search or for other purposes such as determining the validity of a school for post-military service.

CHAPTER ELEVEN
Growing LinkedIn Outreach

Now that a transitioning veteran has completed a fully vetted profile and has made some great connections, it's important to keep some relevancy on this profile.

A great deal of information has been written on this topic. As a LinkedIn executive coach, I tell business leaders that they should try to spend fifteen minutes every day to go through their LinkedIn feeds. To me, this is a productive use of my time, and it replaces the many networking functions I once attended. I glean helpful information by being open to new, relevant ideas and concepts expressed by and among the nearly 4000 people who have connected with me.

Michael Quinn, a retired Army sergeant major, recently posted some great goals in a recent LinkedIn post. To me, they represent the basic involvement every transitioning vet needs for a successful career transition.

First, Quinn said people should reach out to three new people a day. A vet can use the LinkedIn search tool to find people in their industry or those who share their interests. Once someone is identified, a person seeking a connection should create and personalize each request.

Next, when someone who is a connection posts something of value, you should, at the very least "like" it, Quinn said. However, taking what noted social media author Erik Qualman said, you should also "share it forward." If a connection posts an article or thought that really resonates, you can also repost it.

Finally, every vet should write their own posts on topics related to their experiences and their interests. I see too many people who really get stuck here. They want a perfect post and they will wait weeks to upload it. By then, the topic has become outdated. Be thoughtful and smart, and always re-read your post – before you hit the "post" button.

I make it a habit to check my LinkedIn messages at least once a day. I have connected this email-like feature to my business inbox, and I have also set the LinkedIn connectivity feature that enables me get alerts on my phone.

LinkedIn shows every one of its members the name and background of people who have stopped by to visit my profile. Appropriately, I review their profile, and if I sense that we might have a reason to connect, I send them an Inmail or a connection request.

I typically write something like:

> *"Thanks for taking the time to visit my profile. I looked at yours, and I would like to connect with you."*

That little tactic has opened many doors for me.

Lastly, LinkedIn embraces both interactivity and purpose. When someone posts an article or comment, it's important to react to those comments. Yes, while there are some people who simply like to show their brains or wit on LinkedIn, I've found that the remaining 99-percent of those who respond to a post have something worth noting.

If transitioning vets take fifteen important minutes every day with those tactics, it will shape their profile's personality into one that will create some wonderful and relevant connections. This transition growth thinking goes against the typical thought process one learned from their first day of basic training. I admit that it can be hard for most vets to express their thoughts in these interactive forums. Still, when veterans take a proactive role with their LinkedIn profile, it will provide them with the hidden opportunities not found in other networking channels.

Acknowledgement

As any author can tell you, a book needs a lot of help and exceptional inspiration.

I want to thank my friend, Cedrick "Doc" Brown for his help in pushing this project forward. Along with Tom Cuthbert and my Vistage board, they pushed this project forward.

I want to thank Bruce Colthart, this project's graphic designer; my son, Pete and especially my bride of almost 20 plus years, Jackie.

Photo credits:

Page 5 | Courtesy, U.S. Marine Corps

Page 7 | Courtesy, U.S. Air Force

Page 8 | Courtesy, U.S. Air Force

Page 11 | Courtesy, U.S. Navy

Page 17 | Courtesy, Command Sergeant Major Judd Reno

Page 18 | Courtesy, Army First Sergeant Claudia E. Barros

Page 18 | Courtesy, U.S. Air Force

Page 21 | Courtesy, U.S. Marine Corps

Notes

Notes

Notes

Notes

Notes

Notes

CPSIA information can be obtained
at www.ICGtesting.com
Printed in the USA
BVHW06s0926190918
527787BV00007B/30/P